Pain in the Sass®
I enjoy a glass of wine each night for its health benefits. The **other** glasses are for my **witty** comebacks and flawless dance moves

I work so I can afford the amount of alcohol required to continue going to work
Pain in the Sass®

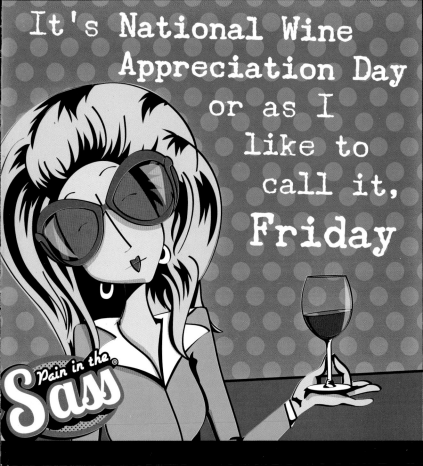

People say that I abuse **alcohol**. But I've only ever spoken **very highly** of it

Pain in the Sass®

This edition published by Ravette Publishing 2016.

Ravette Publishing Limited
PO Box 876
Horsham
West Sussex RH12 9GH

ISBN: 978-1-84161-397-0

Printed and bound in India by Replika Press Pvt. Ltd.

It doesn't matter if the glass is half empty or half full. There is **clearly** room for **more** wine

Pain in the Sass®

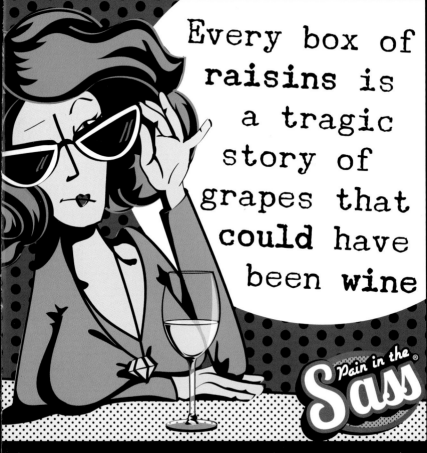